Paul

Enjoy yourself
your poetry

Gus Wilhelmy

Listening to *Music* Within

GUS WILHELMY

Archway Publishing books may be ordered
through booksellers or by contacting:

Archway Publishing
1663 Liberty Drive
Bloomington, IN 47403
www.archwaypublishing.com
844-669-3957

ISBN: 978-1-6657-1860-8 (sc)
ISBN: 978-1-6657-1858-5 (hc)
ISBN: 978-1-6657-1859-2 (e)

Library of Congress Control Number: 2022902320

Print information available on the last page.

Archway Publishing rev. date: 02/03/2022

Foreword

I'm certainly no expert on poetry, but I think some of your poems are quite good. These are the ones that impressed me most (in no particular order):

> "Mirabile Dictu"; "Morning Cranes"; "Morning Swan, My Shadow"; "Never Tomorrow"; "Now, Never Tomorrow"; "No Response"; "Closer than Air"; "The Endless Wait"; Aged Parents in Love"; "Death for the Living"; "Gone"; "In Pieces"

The poems that captured something in nature, such as "Morning Cranes" and "Morning Swan," reminded me that poets *pay attention*. In other words, poets see in ways that most of us don't. They have a kind of contemplative gaze that does not project the ego on the world but rather receives the world as it is. In short, they let the beauty and goodness of things be revealed to them. In that respect, poets counsel us to slow down, to pay attention, and to see the wonder and beauty that is before us every day if we only had eyes to see. Simone Weil spoke of prayer as a matter of paying attention. The English philosopher and novelist Iris Murdoch said that goodness begins in vision, in the rare capacity to see things the way they are rather than as we need them to be. She contrasted that with fantasy, which for her meant bending the world to ourselves. That's why she said so often what we call love is more the work of fantasy (we love others insofar as they meet our needs and fit our plans) rather than love being an expression of reverent attentiveness.

Other poems you wrote, Gus, lift up our deep need for intimacy, for relatedness, but how fragile these can be, and how we can destroy the very things we most need. In this respect, these poems made me think that poets probe the deepest recesses of our natures. They probe all the complexities and contradictions about us. So many of the last stanzas of the poems pack an emotional wallop, a confrontation with the truth. For example, "My Shadow" ends with these words: "As midnight kills that wish / When you vanish always; / I beg you truly hold / And keep me close in dark, / But you dismiss my pleas."

The closing lines of "No Response"—"leaving tombs of silence where / no gentle love-words penetrate; nor rejection slips impregnate; silence muzzles all that's humane"—reminded me of the soft cruelties of life and how they erode our souls and spirits. It made me think that soft cruelties can be much harder to endure than the more obvious vicious cruelties.

I loved the final lines of "Closer than Air": "Then both of us climb / The slopes of hope / Clutching ropes of love." The image of clutching to love was so powerful to me, so true. It's an example of how poets can convey in a few words the exact form of human experience, or they can present that experience to us so that we see it more clearly, more truthfully.

The "Endless Wait" made me think of the year I taught at the University of Scranton. When I left the Passionists in July 1997, I headed to Scranton to teach one year in the theology department there. Because of the distance from Chicago, I only saw Carmella a few times. But your poem brought to mind how, when she came to visit me that year, I was so anxious to see her, so excited, that I would leave my apartment well in advance of her arrival and wait expectantly, so eagerly at the Scranton/Wilkes-Barre airport. I would watch every person coming off the plane, my heart pounding for her.

"Death for the Living," "Gone," and, "In Pieces" were wrenching because they were so honest in conveying the terrible pain that accompanies the end of relationships. The emptiness, the kind of death-like feeling that comes upon us when relationships end was perfectly conveyed in lines like, "Bedrooms seeped with loneliness /

night-chairs sadly vacant stretched/their arms to embrace in hope/a love that they once knew well."

The same sense of desolation came through "In Pieces" with mention of "hoped razed." It brought to mind that good poetry has to be honest, that it cannot be afraid of speaking the truth, but that speaking of the truth is a means of teaching something important, sharing something important with the reader. There was a raw honesty to those poems that dealt with the end of a relationship, but that very honesty, I think, enables a healing.

So many of Gus's poems confirmed that poets see deeper and more truthfully; they see the connection between the inner and the outer. They also remind us that there is beauty to be revealed everywhere, including in some very unexpected places. Poetry helps us see the grace in the ordinary.

Paul Wadell PhD
Professor Emeritus of Theology and Religious Studies
St. Norbert College
De Pere, Wisconsin

Introduction

My main question is this: "How does a poet listen to the world as other?" The question may seem mysteriously complex. Yet the query simply asks how a poet listens first before he or she shares the music. Poetry is metaphors singing a music of what the poet hears in the world out there and within, which is caught by another's ears.

The poems that follow often deal with that which impacts the ordinary person. My poems deal with simple down-to-earth things like highway guardrails, brass of tacks, or rugs kids jump up and down on. Poems are always written to be heard and listened to. The poems' verbal music reveals unpretentious songs or melodies I euphemistically call my poetry.

A poem reveals what the poet hears. Many of the poems to follow are little neighborhood bands sharing music with others. The poems highlight music sharing modest truths of swans in love or of a morning crane grabbing fish. Poetry imparts what the world inside and outside sings to us.

The poetic journey does not consist of finding new suns or moons or stars but in discovering new ears to gain new insights into what is real to the self. Poetry is wisdom found after a journey only a poet can take. No one can take that journey for the poet. Poetry is special. It's a mirror in which one can see beyond the self and catch the other bringing new meaning in a new language.

I can always discern what's good and not so good in the poetry of others. As for my own poetry, I'm clueless. The primary reason I write is to reveal myself to others, so I better understand the "who" I am. The words once on paper give me an insight into what I'm hearing while driving down the roads of life. And, of course, when you're reading and listening to my poetry, I hope you'll gain some insight into yourself and maybe even a deeper understanding of you.

My poems listen to love, charming ladies, nature, squirrels, old rugs, spectacles, bars, cranes, swans, a winter night. My assumption, after eighty-six years in life, are these lyrical endeavors help me to grasp, empathize with, and have compassion for others while valuing myself.

No poem is long. Nor do the poems share my personal history in Minnesota, where I grew up during the Great Depression in inner city St. Paul or on a St. Paul farm in the mid-forties feeding leghorn chickens and plowing with horses who knew rows and furrows better than the farm boy. Nor does my poetry reflect years as a Catholic monk and priest or cofounding Safer Foundation, a nonprofit in Chicago, Safer Foundation, to help men and women coming out of prison find a road back to recovery via decent jobs. Nor does my poetry deal much with forty-five married years, my son and daughter and son- or daughter-in laws along with seven marvelous grandchildren.

So what does poetry mean to me? Before all else, poetry is more than a hobby for fun. It's a way of life, a spiritual journey guided by the gods of literary insight. Albeit I know I'm not a poet of any significance, like a Shakespeare or Dante, nonetheless I offer up my everyday meager skills to the divinities of art. Poetry's truly a bread-and-water necessity that provides survival for the artist. Every poem reflects a felt encounter set in imagistic metaphoric language mirroring an experience that the poet feels a need to share. In a way, through poetry, the poet hopes to reveal unseen metaphysical truths hidden deep down reality. For me that reality is always very unassuming in the practical nuts and bolts of life.

But most important, I see poetic sharing as something very unique. Nelle Harper Lee in *To Kill a Mockingbird* felt that people see what they look for and hear what they want to listen to. I believe my poetry is hearing what I listen to. I deeply crave to listen to others as they are not as I want them to be. My poems eavesdrop nonjudgmentally on others as other. These poetic endeavors listen in order to understand and not to respond. Whether the poem is about a chirping bird in spring or old guys in a bar, it seeks to listen to the other, not an inner self needing to reply to what it wants to hear. The poet's destination is not a place; it's a new way to eavesdrop and discover the genuine essence of the other as other.

The poems in this book could be classified in two groups: one more classical and a second more modern. The classical group hits heavily "style." These poems emphasize rhythm, meter, rhyme, verbal patterns of stressed and unstressed syllables necessary for the lyrics of poetic song.

Other poems touch modernity and are often prosaic. Over the years, I've asked many poets if they understood the difference between prose and modern poetry. They struggled to define a variance. Many weren't certain there existed any precise definition that makes modern poetry distinct from modern prose. Yet I always felt special verbal music in a new linguistic syntax gives poetry its elite artistic touch. That music, with alliteration and assonance in the precision of crisp melodic language empowered with action verbs, brings meaning that cannot be found or heard in the prose of even our greatest prose writers.

The musical language of poetic composition is found in moments of awe or wows emanating in the listening experience. The topics of poetic undertakings enclosed are a city waking up, cranes standing statuesque by a lake at evening tide, occurrences at bars, a biting night, beyond COVID-19, a shadow coming and going, Chicago's slums, squirrels in trees, Stalin toppled, winter's night, and WWII's everyday people and their "doings" away from a war front.

Poets hear things differently, and sometimes in a special way, when their utterings voice aphorisms and wisdom found in listening to understand, not to respond. Sure, my poetic endeavors have great limitations. But for some reason, poets always yearn to share the music they've heard. Most of all, hopefully I'll get the thrill of hearing your voice once or twice in life saying to me, "Wow, Gus, that's a great poem you've written. It says so much to me! It really hits home deeply."

In conclusion, I hope I've caught in poetry's music what I've heard lyrically listening to understand the other in the world outside.

As a poet, I want to reveal such. I trust my lyrical labors of love reflect what I've picked up listening to the world out there. Maybe then poetic music can help listeners hearken to a unique spirit penetrating a world way beyond the self.

I trust my poetic utterances will encourage understanding of all that's poetic out there. Sure, my poetry works hard to impart wisdom. Appreciation of the other as other, however, makes everything blossom; self-centered absorption makes poetry wither and die. Poetry can make us better listeners and more sensitive to the worlds inside and out. The poet as a skillful musician invites others to listen to a music especially about the world around us. The poet is a conductor who orchestrates what he or she has heard while listening to a world beyond self and then putting such into magical notation called poetry. Poetry shares a linguistic music metaphorically expressed in down-to-earth tones that soar us beyond all concrete realities into spiritual and metaphysical realms.

Contents

A Baby Song

There within that chamber space
beneath your mother's heaving heart,
you quickened with a special beat
in love's alarmed and panicked wait.
Then breaking from your breathless night,
striking with such fluent thunder,
she shouts your rhythmic songs of fright.

Your silver shrieks that echoed strife
in no way lightninged fear in her;
while cradling you as special, hers
with tears that streamed so fast and bright,
your mother's pain was now a blur
with roses raining from her eyes
amidst your melody of cries.

A Birth in Chorus

The early ending of winter
in March brought scrawny cries
of birds to his straining ear.

The sun at six arose,
splattering élan on snows,
catching sounds in rays.

He knew he'd heard them,
those cries at daylight or before
of larks In March's wind.

A bit of ventriloquism,
charming echoes
humming winter's end.

Those tiny strains at first
then burst to fullest choir,
streaming with colossal sun.

Resounding in a choral piece,
now so near was nature's song
that winter sings to spring.

A Drenching October—2018

It was the month
    it never stopped raining;
it was the month autumn leaves
    in shredded, colored splats just plopped
mucus-thick on murky swamps;
    it was the month that cowered deer
as guns in rapid fire alarmed
    their refuge yet antlers never stirred;
it was the month we stalked and shivered,
    drenched in sodden clothes as alley cats
that month in hunt for hopes unseen;
    it was into that autumn storm my son and I
trudged knee-deep in the muck
    past logs split-wide by winter's-axe;
it was the month of high-water floods
    in revenge against those who sought
    their prey hiding in the nature cave.
Yes, it was the month
    it never stopped raining.

All Facts

We easily miss brass in tacks
or sober daily scoops of truth
in diapers, dirt, tomato paste,
banana peels, and paper plates.

These mark and amazingly tell
in diamonds' hidden facets,
unnoticed and un-signaled,
detailing subtle aspects of rock.

The simplicity on guards and rails
that mark and sign our roads and clues
us, alerting on how and why,
matter-of-fact oft shows what's real.

And sometimes lost, we unearth bits
of data on our streets, where lamps
so light the way to common sense
and point out how to find the prompts.

This cunning sincerity hides
among the thorns that roses mask
as simplicity touches real
and grabs the bloody truth at hand.

9/11: Phoenix Smothering in Ash

Skies unsheathe their knives of low-flying planes
that stab their needles into cloth-like buildings,
slowly swelling ground, a groaning casket
with bodies and bones and pieces searing,
smelling, crackling in a deadly fireplace,
with screams and sobs in polysaturated
air as the muddied, corrugated waters
covering a low-laying soot-filled sky,
awaiting more Islamic terror,
crammed with cacophonous clamor and cries,
where lifetimes are but brief moments
getting smoldered in despair-strangling smoke
that garrotes in last hurrahs of stifled hope
every phoenix now smothering in ash.

A Serbian Spring

Plum trees bloom where canons of ethnic hate
burst forth in spring to plow again the earth;
and a lady sixty-eight, in woolen skirt
with sunburnt face, on war-furrowed road waits,
sitting on handbags and her bloodstained cape,
sole remains from years of pain and escape.

With hollow eyes she gazes, staring far,
trembling inside, looking to cling to her
race so routed with shame three weeks prior,
when Croat troops—pouring like hot, black tar
down daisy-white hills in brutal campaign—
gang-raped her village and to her home laid claim.

Smeared with grime from a thousand-year carnage,
she did not bathe for those twenty-one days,
awaiting the bus where gaunt cattle grazed,
and refugee women all herded in rage
had sunk to the mattresses strewing the floors
as victims and the pawns of male game-wars.

Adult Discovery

Children once! Son and daughter! Adults now.
Yes, real burning rains scalding me at times.
Again sunshine promising endless faith
whether tears or hugs, hurt or love, so real.

These reflections now crossed yesteryear's bridge,
where kids on swings no longer fly up down,
laughing as earth and sky go sailing by,
screeching catch-as-catch-can by God and luck.

But now? Reality moves fast-forward to
homeschool, where one's teaching tiny toddlers
to grasp math, the other explaining law
to state police seeking to protect streets.

The school's home for her instructing babes
on how to quickly be smart beyond just fun,
and he implores courts and traffic judges
that common sense be the best rule while driving.

Both spur today's youths and adults to grab
verities in classrooms and streets; and I
return to where the six- and eight-year-olds
swing up and down, shouting nation wisdom.

Afraid

I'm shoulder-deep in the dark,
rushing soul-steeped in fright.

As night endangers me,
blackness engulfs my heart.

Lost on roads, the shadows
turn me into trembling.

Past village clocks I run,
never daring to catch time.

Terrified of phantoms,
I dash past fearsome woods.

Plunging streams that jolt me,
swimming freezing waters.

Then alone and submerged,
I drown in deepest dread.

Ageless Odes

Compulsion never stops
the unending habits
to cram poet hourglass
with metaphoric prose.

I'm sunk in ragged lines full
of thoughtless verbs curdled
in sour word tasting
and poetic gagging.

Wintry lines poetic
leave me harsh and stiff
with icicles of verse
cold enough to blister.

Then, when there are empty nights,
my inner caves are scenes
only of verb nightmares
and bathetic drabness.

How escape constant strain
and disengage iambs,
dactyls, and anapests
causing so much distress?

And how does one catch
again that music magic
or hear chorales in robes
intoning ageless odes?

An Exchange

These kids aren't normal!
They're so different!
Yet their solemn screams
in silence cry, "Look, look
our way, over here because
we'd like to exchange
our wheelchair, walker, cane
for dreams of normalcy,
like you, who everywhere
you go enjoy the pleasure
of people greeting you
and gazing in your eyes
with glowing morning hope
that brings a quiet smile
deep inside; so disregard
our tortured gait, the voice box
or standing frame; just meet
us on the street of need
with warming words and winks
because we're kids who hurt,
who ache to clutch what's real;
but more than in our minds
exists the dream that we're
a member in the stream,
swimming side by side
with you. Aren't we,
aren't we there with you?"

An Old Man

Thinning-gray he scratches and aches,
watching daily markets up-down,
clutching cribbage boards and dreaming
faster than the odds he can peg.

Memory just misplaced a book
about Lincoln's Civil War, while bills
stacking up in fear glare at him,
insisting that he fade away to sleep.

Just an old fart, fussing at night,
needing to pee six times plus three,
putting down broken spectacles,
grousing phones don't ever ring loud.

Knowing gold or silver always
strays his pocket-banks he frets,
flinging tired crutches to the chair,
collapsing asking bed to grab him.

Aware of Bar Sagacity

A bar's in Fergus Falls on Lincoln called Hammered Pete's,
where guys often go to sloosh a beer with pickled eggs
in vinegar and chomp on chips and hear Brad and Hank
complain of wives bitching worse than bosses at work.

Old Joe over there, quietly munching onion rings, let me say
he may be high but paints surreal stuff better than Dali did;
or Bud and Ed pounding air with fists as Molly's serving them
are yakking about prices of cheese and meat at Walmart.

And nearby at bar's end, violet smells on Suzy attract
noses of guys to slide a few beers down her way
and soften life without her kids for a drinking mom
the judge said only lives for booze, not her brood.

But don't say a word about this or about our bar at all;
and don't waste time trying to find why it's necessary
because everyone needs listening to, not just hearing,
and whiskey brings some sagacity when life's just pain.

August's Lake

A sweltry August smothers Lake of the Woods
as cresting waves crash against whitened shores
mile-high with jagged black-ridged granite
of Precambrian rock sacred to Cree,
Ojibwe, habitat for pelicans,
and piping plovers, swans; a beauty spread
in grand immortal sweep, sanctuary
where one stands in awe and feels spears of fear
while watching woodland caribou or bear
limned with power share their beauty-danger.

But look, look up yonder into heaven;
behold the eagle circles in sky on wings
of flying ribbon bands so white in streams
as wilderness stirs hope that God, who walked
the waters once, now treads impressively
His skies and paints His shores in green and black
with aspen, pine, and birch outdoing eagle flights
o'er head, while signet pools below become
the home of fish and other water creatures
as nature flaunts her ever splendid scenes.

Awakening

And if the moon must always
go and leave me cold in fear,
how can I sate a soul's hunger
if every eve she seems to fade
so even her mentor, the sun, says,
"Don't waste time being so fickle
waiting for her bread and meat
when sunlight and heat are what's
necessary, and the moon just loves
you and quits and maybe won't return
tomorrow eve, so why do you crave
her, are you just a fool fantasizing want?"

So should I just talk to the moon,
letting her know how much I care,
begging her to clutch me,
hold me tight in her feeling light,
love me deeply as she should,
be at my side at night for thousands of
hours when I'm lost in bleakest wood,
and could she teach me how to love,
grabbing me and telling to catch whispers
about so much to receive from Miss Moon,
sharing her light with me even at night,
making life for me when all is blackest?

So should the moon be guide and friend,
holding my hand to help me detect
ways through loss when everything's gone
wrong, and will she lead me dizzy in dark,
blinded in fear when fingers can't be seen
groping to feel the warmth of any place,
unable to find keys to my home, a space
where lying down I'd be able to decide
what's next and if seeking the moon,
asking her presence would lighten ways
answering questions in mysterious mist
clouding the path home in doubt's blackness?

Aware of Nothing

At home or on the road,
he wends in feckless fantasy
beyond the weed and drugs
on streets where women ply
their trades, and tiny tots
just pee in rags of indigence.

The beggars plea with cars
for coins to clang their cups,
while flies on puppy dung
buzz in espionage;
yet he never hears moans
nor catches straits of strife.

He misses the grass unkempt
on veterans' graves and's closed
to violence in base-clef thunder
of the murders last night,
or clotheslines hanging rags
of pain on jungle-city streets.

He soars in heaven's bliss,
completely free of winds from
slums and shattered windows
as he licks candy-cotton,
drinking wine in floods
of toasts with lady lust!

Best by Nature

I took a road traveled less,
gazing at the splendid sea,
feeling on her sandy shores
softest cotton 'neath my feet.

Comely clouds in crowds above,
I viewed dancing in heaven,
bidding one watch their ballet
prancing in white against blue.

Then pounding, quick-cresting waves
make their peaking white salutes,
sending swans in flying sprays
winging past the palm tree lanes.

Learning fast values beyond,
grasp these natural treasures,
brings an awesome wonderment
only nature hides then presents.

Bethlehem: A Sinful City

A town in love,
a sinner's place to be,
a luscious night for all
in clutching lusty hugs.

While pressed against
a girl's breast, divinity
quietly in linen bands
sleeps so soundly.

The God in infancy
brings naked tininess
to Bethlehem as God
becomes us, one with sin.

Birthing

My mom would birth
a baby boy;
she shouldn't though
for doctors claimed
the battleground
was her being,
and the infant
would murder her
in St. Luke's ward,
declaring war,
seeking but death
as her faith wept,
"Holy Mary,
Mother of God,
don't take my son,
your second son,
he is yours too,
and please dismiss
this deadly threat."

Swiftly, my mom,
hearing infant
cries, just pressed him
softly, careful,
love pouring tears,
pleading for all
to come and see
and greet the babe

unfeigned to share
her beaming joy
and gently touch
her firstborn son,
her wetting god,
her diapered dream,
her "now" come true.

Black Cat

You're the smoothest blackest cat
always here, then always not,
ever slinking into darkness,
searching for a place to be such.

Withdrawn—a ghost invisible,
slipping somewhere into secret
lairs, you completely disappear
in a shroud of ebony curls.

Unseen, you crack my heart open,
one side questing its fleeting hint
of you; the other craving eyes,
panther piercing, so enticing.

Vanished, you utterly awaken
everything that's asleep in me,
where among the walking dead, I'm
ever ready to come back live.

Sure, your silver-black stirs up hope,
not rage, that you'd again be ball
of mellow warmness in my arms
enfolding you, a blessed guest.

Then night turns moments into dread,
and absence makes my heart less fond,
when your departure proves the truth:
Souls grow only when pain's sharp keen.

Can I Go Inside?

Will you be the key and unlock
your heart and precious soul and share
your cherished home where I can go
and hide to throw away life's dread?

I yearn my God would share largess
within that treasure chest of you
where I could hide inside and be
so tightly locked within you there.

Your air, it seems is safe to breathe,
removing years of choking gloom,
that gives despairing darkness hope
the bracing atmosphere ensures.

A money prize has no import
when value in your treasury
will lend your eyes and golden care
to cut the losses steeped with fear.

I trust at last you'll be the rock
on which I stand securely strong
to ward off waves of crashing threat
and have your love caressing warm.

Chicago's Dream in '68

Tranquil in spirit,
the city stretches awake,
embracing its skies
of hushed-morning peace,
bringing overnight violence
the kindness of dawn.

Sharp knives, pungent flesh
trafficked a night of shame
as Chicago spilled out lives
in potholes of bloody woe,
leaving last evening replete
with color-hemorrhaging hate.
Yet last night swims in hope
anew as morning silver
glints off 'scraper panes,
and faith in passers below
drinks unquenching drafts
of warming love for the day.

City Awakens

Outside the foggy arms
enwrap the city limbs,
and you don't appear;
you're just being there,
waiting to be seen
in streets buried black,
just aching for light
to cut away the blur
that wraps in hazy mist
each cable stretching out
its lines like sprouting trees.

Suddenly, you come awake
as morn arrives and begins
to undress you in light;
and eyes amazed now see
there's nothing to hide
as furtively you glance
around your bedroom
while intruding hands
just pull away the covers
and shout, "City's alive!"

Closer than Air

Dear love, my love,
you are a candle,
a flame that always burns.

You're torrents in darkness
with rays that never die
or ever dim.

You're closer than the air;
you're the pulsing heart
that beats my blood within.

Oh, your spirit door's
a womb as you await
an entry I so crave.

In splendid candidness
our hearts do comingle
in oceans of warmth.

Yes, we plunge and drown
and lose our lives in oneness
that infinity surely owns.

Then both of us climb
the slopes of hope,
clutching ropes of love.

Conundrum

Sometimes it's difficult to distinguish
Between the self and one's God
And decide what's right or wrong, up or down,
As one rides reflectively the merry-go-round
Of conundrums that just compound on how
A man in la-la land becomes a foolish clown.

It always seems so clear to everyone out there
To know who's God and that He's never Jack or Jill.
Before one talks or ever walks, one knows the real
Between omniscient need and lusty dream,
But never is so clear on how divinity achieves this
Or gives support to hope beyond the reveries.

One won't deny the power of omnipotence
Nor being trapped between a dream and need
That bridges waters of divinity and humanity,
Spanning every overpass of day and bleakest night,
Where drugs and joints and all things so rebellious
Finally get resolved in caressing precious love.

Death for the Living

He closed the somber book
of names to pen his own
but could not do it now
for death had stopped his heart
barraged by her demise.

Her silence echoed back
no tranquil sounds at all,
and lips that kissed him once
now pressed just burning angst,
enwrapping him in loss.

Her words he could not hear,
nor gentle calming tones,
no whispers; just aching
and paining hope for her,
but no lark song was sung.

And driving home that eve
everything seemed taken,
demanding that he stop
to sink in hellish hush
and drown in her silence.

Divorced Love

It isn't marriage at all!
It's love stripped of old
torn shreds and threads
of tawdry hopes getting tossed
in shades of bleakest gray;
illusions that shout aloud
love isn't an alpine peak.

But remember, in Vegas terms,
hope shoots crap all the time,
when seven comes eleven
and doesn't break the bank;
then appears combinations
on how to dial safes to grab
purest gold that never rusts,
which happens when you lose
the bet but win all the rest.

This dawning truth instructs
old buffs not to Sherlock,
seeking clues hid beneath
a couch or in a bra
or even in Grandpa's chest;
brimful with tenderness
as fresh as lambs in birth,

at last new zeal treads woods
ne'er trod before by foot,
with ethos that compels
a clutching truth to seal
and feel real love in divorce.

Do You Ever Listen?

When her eyes are oceans
and sadness crimps her voice,
her depression smolders
with hurt he cannot hear
in aching quests that weep,
"Do you ever listen?"

His ears catch frequencies
as pillow-pounding pleas
lament her hopeful tries
for him to hear desires
refraining all the time,
"Do you ever listen?"

A senseless charade;
he never sees candles
sobbing dimly at night
nor catches the ache
and sadness in a plea,
"Do you ever listen?"

And when he feels her cries
and sees them in her eyes,
he knows her womanhood
has milk his soul implores
yet he can never grasp.
"Do you ever listen?"

Dying to Live in 2021

The world's different now than once it was
as sharing goes today beyond tidbits
of crumbs, as value-banquets nourish deep
the heart that hungers for food and meaning.

Of course, worlds seem confused in spite of dreams
since blind and deaf and walking dead just stare,
complaining as they wring their hands in loss
while feeling the new now is naught for most.

They inexplicably ask what's real,
and yearn with tears of joy for what is,
as larks abound and soar in heaven's song
with chants in lovely winding ribbonry.

An echo plays back that the worst is past
when compassion with its refraining mores
exterminates a once-tenacious death,
and life now hugs new love in godly clutch.

Fear Pandemic

No explaining this pandemic;
reporters make me scared as hell.

It's chilling when you're clueless,
and no one knows which way to turn.

Sunk in terror upset by the virus,
it's death at eighty-six in coffin's hell.

Dread jangles nerves, hearing, "Stay home,
wear masks, social distance, vaccinate.

Watch constantly, wash your hands,
don't touch others, banish groupings."

Lying in bed alone with the desert cactus,
no God, no help, no hand can soothe.

Red lights flashing fast proclaim,
"Stop, look, grab the power."

Guardedly I search and look what's there
when someone answers, "Power's within."

Fishing Dream

On this evening, his head savors fish
    In sights of lakes and seas,

where jumping thousands are but frank data
    verifying wishing,

and dreams of catches in hopeful millions
    slip into moonlit nets

while everyday fishermen like he
    in fantasy eschew facts,

but he among distant stars just teems
    with fishing truth in trance.

Friendship

You are fierce.
You're fragile.
You're faithful
diffidence.

You demand
rains that seep.
Yet drought can
make you sprout.

Naught scares you.
For you state
when you're lost,
you'll be found.

You aren't me.
Yet you are.
You're open
secrecy.

George Floyd Lives

Is he dead or alive; does it matter?
Can men in blue just destroy life with knees
crushing necks of anyone to steal breath?

Yet George, it seems, never ceases to breathe
but endlessly survives in everyone
amazed at him who always lives on slum streets.

The hailing hearts believe and scream new trust,
and youth now shout with hope from pushing crowds
as women vowing tears just clutch him near!

Alive, yes, all alive they screech in screams
for their murdered icon resurrected
is meekness, gleaming soft humility.

Endowing deep both black and white who weep,
new trust his spirit strives to bring to life
reviving hope on 38th and Chicago.

The answers righteously self-evident
will ever cancel lies of killing knees,
while concrete always shouts aloud, "He lives."

Hands That Speak

Slender beauty, long and sleek, speaks
in traces brushing as they bring
true passion-chances, stirring hope
in tones that rouse his tempting pleas.

Brushing fingers wipe her eyes dry,
while hunting for the bonding drop
that clutches with a whisper-soft
in tips that rouse inviting quests.

Nail paint purrs quietly on hands,
like hummingbirds suggesting search
in lovely flights for hidden truths
beneath the sparking tints aglow.

Her fingers gently push so deep
to reach a moment when in thrusts,
with love, they beckon one to grasp
the warming clasps of dreams turned real.

Her Eyes: A Doorway

As she descends the oaken staircase,
I can't forget the sharp white collar lifting off
the dress of Japanese silk, where magic grace
frames alluring eyes gleaming mystic smiles.

Sesame gazes so appeal and loft one
to playful places where joy abides as children
flying kites and dancing in sparkling lights,
touching gently strings in clouds of lovers.

Their looks are Eden streaming a new Eve,
bringing wooing cries of silence before sin,
flowing to embrace what comes alerting touch
canalling, yearning, longing of fierce want.

Their regard, a doorway to beauty now grows
in nights of feeling wild hope, provoking what
no one knows but those aching to cross
the threshold into an anxious embrace.

Her First Night's Love

How much would woeful worry choke her heart?
Loving-- then crossing fingers hoping
and praying inside—fearing each next hour.

Had boy-on-girl love enwrapped her dream
in real--or would she just await a lover's scorn
and anger to blame her loose and wanton ways?

Had curtains lifted where she had staged her skit
with love—but without a plot--without a score?

At first, the play re-played glowing memories:
 A night
 A boy
 A kiss
 A lip lock
 A fastened tongue
 A breast
 A lay
 A magic moment's clasp.

But memories soon had turned to dark within:
 An aching heart,
 After shame,
 Bolted hopes,
 Left-overs,
 A sour taste,
 A messy dress.

Her car alone drove that night:
      No encore--
      No boy around—
      No sweet after kiss—
      No clutching of each other!

At home, she buried empty hope and placed
her evening rose in waterless despair
her vase now held in a drooping soul.

And she recalled upon a pillow hollow
what could have been that was before.
but now no more! For all the music's dead!

Her Music in Scent

Like music played in fantasy on keys
of yesteryear, today my fingers glide
upon your face, your sensuous ear

and streaming eyes; you're scenting
clean and warm just sings a note
that can be heard and throbs and beats

a rhythm like floating Japanese silk
that stirs the strains of anthems
within the touch, and maiden sirens

plucking chords that make pure melody
as she stands in pristine charm
in pleasure's parlor, where Ovid stays

and, bathed in primal passion, she mingles
desire and dance and a quivering harp
that quavers, awaiting clashing cymbals

when raucous refrains without shame
become her bawdy trumpet blare,
uplifting the night into strumpet play,

and, anon, a symphony written afresh
on musical sheets finds springtime lays
with scented hosannas streaming in lace.

His Spectacles

The saucer near his morning paper
often holds his glasses; trimmed
with silver, rimmed in black that seems
to gleam, the sun upon the page
and makes the print so bold and bright
it almost shouts the news at him.

And when he's sipping coffee hot,
and toast is somewhat breakfast burnt,
his glasses find in scrambled eggs
with well-mixed Tater Tots, a spot
of sacred bits that's there, and tells
in hidden hints what'll start his day.

At work, he brims again coffee cups
and puts his glasses on to read
a note his secretary placed;
then spectacles shout out demands
his wife makes that he stop tonight
at Macy's before home ASAP.

At last, as sun slips low out west
and specs remind him work's finished,
and from his drowsy head delete
the need to read more pressing stuff,
his glasses now declare must wait
and delay early next-day faire.

Hummingbird

I am the hummingbird;
the hummingbird is me.
A tiny powerhouse,
250 wing beats a minute.
Heart in flight on flowers,
nectar-fueling beak,
all humming in power—
wing, heart, and pace.

Flying dynamics,
every bit of me
darting, weaving, hovering,
clinging air,
changing directions,
instantly reverse
without skipping beats.
Nature at its best.

How I long to be
a myriad species,
biomechanics play,
a flight in evolution,
magic beauty miracle
flashing here and there,
abiding hummingbird,
that hummingbird I see.

Hushed Dignity

You are my morning cannonade, brightness
dissipating last eve's lingering aches;
you are my sunup fountain of gentle spray,
leaving me touching nakedness and day.

You are my garden enwrapping in vines,
my pond of open lilies in flower,
my high-noon hammock of love inviting one
to soul-mate and embrace in pleasure's sun.

You're my pine shimmering a sunset sky,
my beautiful, dainty Queen Anne's Lace;
no chameleon hides in your brown eyes,
only friendship's gift as its glowing prize.

Your hands in a special way share roses,
encircling thorns that never penetrate
or cut or try to tear asunder
that beautiful bond of trustful wonder.

Ice-Cream Dreams

Down alleys near the ghetto streets,
He passes junkyards crammed with trash
And treats the kids who dart and dash
To streams and dreams of all ice cream.

Clanging the hood with tinny tunes,
He shoves his frozen ice-cream cart
Among the little urchin larks
Who flit and fly like bouncing balloons.

With songs to which they tap and twirl,
He plays his four-wheeled music box
That romps away despondent tots
In squeals that plea for dairy swirls.

They dance and beg to trade their dimes
For jumbo cones of graham crackers,
Playing their eyes with triple-stackers
That pound their hearts beyond their cries.

Pink-ribboned girls and gypsy boys
In Nikes cheer their ice-cream man
Who puts his cones in begging hands,
Awaiting mounds of ice-cream joy.

In Pieces

Ruined marriage everywhere,
leaving dreams echoing down
halls that once had been
places beaming love's touch.

Stinging lies of yesteryear
incise the heart and leave
remnants of no self-worth
shredded by two-faced words.

Broken promise, hope razed,
shattered marriage strewn
fantasy in pieces
scattered by divorce.

Alas, stop memories of
moonlit nights holding hands,
reaching out, embracing
hearts in perspiration.

Yes, best bid goodbye, and
stop blowing lifeless faith
in ash that can't enflame
rotted pledges of toxic wood.

Lady Bee

A queen, sliver-blue,
searches daffodils
as effusive spring
with hope rushes in on
relentless March winds;
as buzzing bees,
after drinking flowers,
fill the honeycomb
for their faultless queen.

Her Majesty hums,
awaiting her ladies'
daily return from
their buzzing labors
getting pollen-pay from
geranium stamens,
creating decent combs
where nectar is stored
by an all-female workforce
that colonizes communities
having the queen in command
down by the iron gate,
where flowers in bouquets
orchestrate in springtime
a symphony directed flawlessly
by a majestic lady.

Love and Intimacy

Swiftly love in lightning flashes,
brilliant moments rare with you.

Math always makes us equal two,
but you remain the special one.

Nighttime shines your star upon us,
calming storms ever crashing ashore.

Loneliness dashes far away,
havened in bonds you bring this eve.

Intimacy undercover
flourishes in this newest DNA.

Soothing "must", as norm, constrain you,
penetrating veins with belief.

Love beyond deceit and lying
finds its bliss now enfolding us.

Learning to Weep Joy

Exploiting her way with baseball grace
in disciplined skill without swagger or sway,
she robs young batters of striking power,
assigning ladies to weeping showers.

Who she is and beyond she will ardently tell
as she kills guilt better than chefs make bisque,
then returns to computer games after bursting
taboos as well as the masks of social space.

Without making an unseemly show, she lets
her devotion in canine classes unfold
a career of hope around puppy pursuits
as hugs help her dog moms bring forth the new.

Yes, she breaks everything too feminine
while brimming with play and job ambitions,
her eyes gleaming tears for pop-star idols
strum at her heart as only Jonas can.

Mirabile Dictu

Infancy's a mystery unknown,
where eternity finds in cosmic space
obscurity in time and place,
evolving in wiggling toes and fingers.

Divinity disguised in infant-wraps
just lies and hides on earth and hopes
that love converts its sunless nights
to flesh every transcendent day.

Earth so stands amazed at bundled
breath in miracles on sheets that bring
such godliness, which sunk in dreams,
just squirms in covered endless sleep.

Morning Cranes

Like dreams in early morning,
Cranes
Arrive to scan and search for fish.

They stand so statuesque,
As straight as soldiers at attention.
They strut and stride.

Arrows in eyes leering,
They spy for walleye, perch, and prey,
Stalking liquid pillar-stiff.

Their swimming cuisine
They desire to surprise with beaks
About to strike in death.

Thieves stealing
Flopping catches in beaks clasped
To enjoy their breakfast.

Morning Swan

"It's time for work," my watch complains,
yet I can't depart; my heart bids
I wait and watch the morning swan
and script no poem—just stay and gaze.

"Watch her—remain," the inlet pleads,
and listen to water calling,
"Catch her grandeur in nobility,
her sunup majesty steaming out."

My feet then feel a quickened need
to leave for work's most urgent tasks,
while eyes engage her elegance
when seizing morning fish, a catch.

Yes, waters know quite well they flow
everywhere—north, south, east, and west—
but ecstasy holds heart fast and firm
as swan-like beauty swims at morn.

My Shadow

My shadow knows at dawn
The sun will stir up doubts
With questions that pursue,
"Are you with me or are
You with me not at all?"

At noon the sun decides
To wade and swim way out
Into lakes that sparkle
Splendid magnificence,
And you've escaped for good.

Then candles bring on eve,
And you do resurrect,
Appearing everywhere,
Stoking desires that stir
A hope you'll stay all night.

As midnight kills that wish,
When you vanish always,
I beg you truly hold
And keep me close in dark,
But you dismiss my pleas.

No Response

There I was—my email waiting—
knowing I should arrange to lie
in the casket of "no response,"
where a mortuary blackness
engaged in somber timelessness
denies one even day and night
the soundless agony straining
to hear even agonizing "nos"
or feel cuts of rejection slips

yet so much worse than
tinkling crystal no one hears
in noiseless time or quiet
leaving feelings smothered clueless,
aching to get rejection slips,
or be treated like American flags,
stomped and fiercely burned
by insurrectionists in protest,
knowing no fate could be far worse

than being sentenced to death
by emails, so responseless,
creating end and agonizing quiet
and deafness killing, it seems,
any hope of communication
in the tombs of silence where
no gentle love words penetrate
or rejection slips impregnate;
silence muzzles all that's humane.

Not on a Donkey

Unlike his mentor, who came to the city
o'er palms like flowers strewing the way,
Francis, dismayed by the flock he loves,
just walks to his car, a Focus in brand.

A clatter of praise cram-jams his way
with gnarled hands grabbing and greasy
touching his soul, his heart, even sandals,
but ever confessing his own sinful ways.

Like Jesus, this father the icons reject
and statutes declare unsacred and dead;
eschewing accustomed ethereal bows,
he escapes on roads by most untread.

He speaks from pulpits down in the pews
a news devoid of canons and pomp,
and ecclesial codes he gently discards
or puts on shelves for popes more holy.

This new Nazarene enters his city,
a samaritan from a foreign land,
with arms spread wide to godless
and godlike uplifted to his Holy Father.

Now Forever

Dive in now; don't
drown in recall,
seize the moment.
Leap overboard,
swim strong, windward
waves colliding.
Slice present hard,
cutting fiercely
hand over hand.
Never impede
the vision quest
now forever.

On Her Train

A lady, born to travel fast on mod tracks
that males master early in love's exchange,
knowing femininity wants choice and chance
to wave adieu to all social taboos
on journeys where she baggage handles
as porter, chambermaid, and conductor,
showing smiles as clear-cut sole companion
passing through male chicanery and ruse
on Pullmans disguised in equality.

Riding tracks rocking, cracking through the night
past fish docks smelling, blackened cabins, sleep
evading, she knows darkness hides desires;
swelling daring breasts pointing straight ahead
to where beyond joking she must travel
enfolding his hand, embracing his soul,
travels down tracks less traveled but chosen
As goddess of cloth and food and business design,
expressing her views of worlds so global and true.

She moves to and fro out of Eden's puberty,
Eve on a date, her latest excursion with Adam,
Throwing off robes of shame her mind once caressed;
Not sullying the train, journeying now naked,
Breaking at last the crystal glass and ancient pane,
Next to the man she's changed—so utterly changed—
Who champions her feminine sway of power,
Soaring beyond dreams of even an Angelo.

Opinions

Views are not redemptive truths.
They are little more than embers of thoughts
Dying in whitened ash from past debates.
They're blight on flowers once pretty
But have lost freshness in desert air.
Opinions or perceptive proofs—so it seems—
Are a hundred million different views
Sharing where each soul was last eve.

Rain Forever

Drops of rain creation
pouring down morn and eve,

falling early and late,
runnels in forest jade,

stippled droplets streaming
gutters in a thousand trees,

arousing doubt and fear,
soaking deep heart and soul

with dread it'd never end;
this dappled dripping black

holding feelings in trees
furrowed wet with paths

through leaves and green
drenching walk and way

below in floods and fright
that forests would yield naught

but rains that once had saved
the earth and Noah's life.

Request in Dark

Hush, don't say a word!
Darkness urges. Listen!
The shadowed chair over
there stands straight up
with nighties and a dress
as your silhouette glows
in moonlight floods upon
our bed, and I stare with
inhalation, whispering
in longing with hope
against hope that craves
your mouth, voice, tongue;
and all release the reluctance
to sate my starving needs
for your screams and feel
the touch of your soul upon
my lips and clutch your wild
heart in my savage arms
until we join in heaven's bliss
orchestrated in symphonic
moans of two in unison
finalizing soothing peace.

Rug, True Friend

I vacuum your carpet strands,
deeply rooted grass
of cotton, wool, and even rubber,
reminding me of mowing as a kid;
you're tough as Sonny's fist,
a carpet with some weeds,
a lawn unkempt and aching
to touch my board and base,
quickly changing magic looks
for lands of off-white Berber,
where you entertain a bunch
of kids dancing, bouncing fun
leaving smudging prints all over
your patterned galaxies,
colored interwoven circles
always visible at night and day,
scared stiff undersides bringing
much that's ugly, irregular,
to being clean as sheets
that blow in summer winds.

Everything I want is you.
Fresh and chaste. You are here,
engraved to a lovely edge;
no, you're not a sad old rug,
carpet no one wants to prize,

where cats won't squat to pee:
You're truest friendship,
you're Rembrandt,
beautiful brocade I crave
bringing revery to me.

Scared As Hell

Scared I'd die in snow's grave,
deep where many frozen
meet death in cold's anger
with car stuck in snow's clutch,

and fear sends the soul to
bejabbers as jowls clench
windows in blue-black fright
everywhere, and appears

specters so suddenly,
crying for their lives,
stumbling broken moonlit
snows in hopeless cold,

shaking, ragged, shivering,
gasping in clouds of breaths,
stumbling—almost rigid—
confined to winter's shock

as swelling deathly cold
begets the scary sight
of limbs and broken trees
inviting one to die.

She Shares

When you want me to hug your soul,
you find a recipe of dreams
and set out crystal charm and dish
with fares deviously arranged.

If such doesn't fully sway taste
in exquisite ways, you again
prepare your special lover's faire,
the treasured feast of deepest night.

Soul Strained

He teared watching a Corolla fade
away, removing hope
and missed chances to undo
moments squandered.

Kitchen pots and pans were crazed
for her fingers' touch
as half-cleaned cups wept, feeling
stored away and shunned.

The bedroom soaked so empty
as night chairs pled with arms
outstretched aching to caress
and hold what once was theirs.

Strained with want, he labored
to see a thread of far-off road
was more than a funeral hearse
taking her forever from his soul.

Siberian Winter Morn

Last night a floating Siberian shower
Enwrapped in snow every branch and bower.
Enrolling in softness make-believe white,
An ermine-like fur in hoary-frost light,
A fresh morning fleece so lovely to eye
That stirred up inside the outcry of why?
Why does only severely minus night
Bring quick-gold brightness to a nature sight?

The wonder of it—branch and briar and vale—
Only shines when the frozen sharp-toothed gale
Brings death with harshness as it cleans it all
Of grit and grime and a blackened-leaf fall.
For only death lets snowflake the bower
And bring out whiteness in winter's flower.

Springtime

The spirit eagles soar and climb through fluent skies
of innocence,
where blue waters spell loyalty,
and peace renders mountains olive.
The essence of the springtime comes
serene with droplet-morning dews
and lovely rose magnificence
enhancing garden stateliness.
April's grandeur always assails
pretty women and gentlemen,
inviting them walk hand in hand,
reveling in their warmth and dream.

When garden love creates again
a kiss so fixed and lusciously steep,
it blossoms from the heart a grace
that ensures a "Oneness-Portrait."

Squirrels

In winter's frigid clime,
all the working's done
in branches and trees
where squirrels reside.

Detectives in disguise,
Sherlocks seeking clues,
they search for acorn food
hidden yesterday.

Scanning leafless trees,
they look behind each branch
to ensure their hoards
haven't been revealed.

It's never over yet;
they come back to check
as security guarding homes
to know they've done their job.

The DNA of squirrels unknown
as stashers without names
for each other they're strangers
in branches hiding supplies.

Yes, epicenters of coldest peace
even in winter's deadly north,
they maintain lines of command,
keeping squirrel laws of demand.

Stalin Toppled

In Moscow's sculpted grove where Joseph lay
broken in stature, so toppled at night,
shadowed by sainted Basil's domed sight,
I stood bone-drenched on that sodden day,

hearing millions of chanting voices arise
in waves. "A new revolution," they yell,
"Sounds the final knell to your demon-hell
where wars, canals, and five-year designs

killed forty million who died yet survive
your hammer and sickle 'neath this morning sky,
and today stand tall and ask, 'Joseph, why
did you strew our fields, wanting so few alive,

beheading those whose descent you decried,
whose hopes beyond swords now gleamed in their eyes,
reflecting unending victorious cries
destroying the dragon now on its side?'"

That First Crush

At twelve years old, my first heartthrob
just fluttered feathers everywhere
and waltzed a dance of winning tunes
in words that hopes just sing so pure.

But dreams soon sink in saddest plight
as nightfall fills with fatal fear
the paths that wander hopelessly
through woods without a shade of her.

The clocks all tock with distant beats
of loneliness that seep the soul
as Father Time declines to point
the way to find her love or home.

The Endless Wait

A silence cloaks the hazy dusk
in waiting, searching on the tips
of toes, as endless hopes

press and strain to see your face
full of love, so I can sing again
and hear your tones within my soul.

Now darkness drapes my loneliness
with endless magazines to read
and solitaire and cluttered trays,

while echoes promise your return
that pulsate in the drops of rain
now falling on my cottage roof

and streaking windows I peer
through at night, that penetrates within
searching every memory

for you; I'm not the marble cold
nor crystal hard; I am a home
with fireplace and welcoming hearth,

awaiting longingly your flame
with flowing hair against my face
as smiling lips pursue my heart.

Trumpeters' Pledge

Elegance in gait on ice, they stride sure
with legs and feet that seem secure, and then pause
as two just glide in sweetest dreams and hear

the river invites stately royalty
and bid the pair to swim its crystal flows
and catch the famous trumpet blare that hails

its king and queen in beauty unimpaired
to sail the charming winter-liquid climes
in picture-postcard bliss with hope and prayer

for two tuxedos—white with beaks as black
as ebony—to maintain a love pace
on mirrored streams and dignify a bond

that nature's swans engage each other in
before they mate upon their waterway
and bring to spring the prize of courtly care.

Who's Got It Best?

Little golden carp—swimming, floating,
stopping, staring up from your bubbling tank,
breathing, escaping to the other side,
diving to the bottom, then wiggling up—
you slowly glide unblinking as you gaze.

I question in the world what is the best,
inside or out; if I tried to live in there,
I'd die! And vice versa; out here with me
you're dead in flopping minutes in my hand,
gasping as you'd thrash around to breathe.

So you and I do survive inside and out
yet always worry about the other,
who's got it best—in water or in air—
or what comes next for us, our life or death,
and are we meant to only stop and stare?

Winter Cold Is Blue

Winter cold's polar blue
as morning's azure roads
lay out in indigo,
embracing all that's bright.

Sun at noon often spreads
its blue in diamond luster,
a streaming Blue Danube
in a sparkling jewel dance.

Then night brings cold its shades
of gray as sadness warns
that gently changing tints
will crush the blue to death.

Winter's Art

Within that splendid winter scene
presenting snows unfold a sight
that hides inside the white of night,
a loveliness in rhythmic hues.

As nighttime showers spangle earth
with marvels that glitter silken,
the stars spread out upon the snow
where moon lays down its golden coin.

The gentle pawprints rabbits make
show tracks that bare small life is near,
yet dark does not explain how snow
creates such iridescent art.

Winter Solstice

Engulfed by darkness and despair,
the people go within and smother
where artificial light unfair
creates endless mocking summer.

The blackest 'scrapers soaring tall
create on sidewalks far below
a specter that conveys at dawn
how icy lights will harshly grow.

Soon piercing canyons are gripped
with midday's rays as winter lays
her signature in nature's script
across her skies at highest day.

Then, low on winter's western plain,
the quiet shafts so fan and spike
in fading beams that slowly wane
as shades embrace invading night.

Sol Invictus—beacon of life,
minion of hope—we celebrate
your rhythms in the living light
as dying you're renewing faith.

So Much More

My lady's more than I can see,
more than bathrobe or hidden fare;
yet never needles drugs to be
a cunning fox and never hides
her lovely grace to lend an air
of Snow White or Wonder Lady.
She drapes herself in lace and song
with words unheard, only hummed,
a secret aching to be shared,
a daffodil wanting to unfold,
a chutzpah keeping much untold.
A real lady, but so much more!

WWII: '41-'45

WWII rallied souls to fight godly wars.
Block captains, sirens darkened lights at night.
Neighbors traded ration stamps like Vegas.
Soldiers paraded, pants pressed razor sharp.
Five-cent flicks screamed war at kids Saturdays.

Barbershops and grocery stores claimed Mondays.
Victory gardens dotted streets with veggies.
Little boys blue, girls pink pledged allegiance.
School blackboards showed if youngsters understood.
Sundays brought forth church prayer to stop the war.

Radios blared, "Save tin cans for GIs!"
War plants signaled dads made the munitions;
Buses and streetcars carried moms to shop.
Teens felt wartime equaled drugstore ice cream.
This was WWII every day at home.

Your Gift

Found only in giving will you open up
a bowless self—no wrap, just mystery—
and hand me a presence so invisible.
A never-ending hiding evidence of love?

Could you unfold like the water's lily
your secrets way down deep, allowing me
to see the water's floating yellow spread
the sinking stems of green plunging what's real?

Or in you does that gift the spirit sends
consume all the shade and tweak out evil,
so the heart can strain and see blossoming
abound in the grandeurs of sky and sea?

Or do you trail a presence in your wake
of lissome light that surges in the sun,
where waves implode an endless loveliness,
a gift so rare that words can never convey?

Your Smile

Sometimes my day's highlight
comes when garage doors
open wide and you walk in,
smiling wider than the door
with day's success
gleaming in your eyes;
and you embrace
your handsome guy,
covering him with
a smile-squeezing
I-love-you-clinch
and a bear-hug crush.

About the Author

Gus Wilhelmy grew up on a chicken farm, became a Catholic monk, and later an ordained priest. He taught in a seminary and later in universities, and founded one of the nation's largest criminal justice nonprofits. As a married priest, Gus has two children, Rochelle and Todd, and seven grandchildren. His passions include watching his grandchildren grow, fishing, eating tasty cuisine, crafting poetry.

CPSIA information can be obtained
at www.ICGtesting.com
Printed in the USA
JSHW020337270322
24271JS00002B/73